Be bright, be happy, always be yourself!

THE **SUPER CUTE** BOOK OF

MARCELINE SMITH

POP PRESS

初めまして。
僕の名前はモグです。
よろしくね！

CONTENTS

WELCOME TO THE WONDERFUL WORLD OF KAWAII!

Kawaii かわいい translates as loveable or adorable. It became a big trend in Japan from the 1970s, when characters like Hello Kitty started appearing on stationery and accessories, but cute character art has been enjoyed in Japan since at least the early 1900s. The rest of the world has its own cute characters too, but Japanese kawaii went global thanks to Hello Kitty and Pokémon in the 1990s.

Today, kawaii is a big part of Japanese culture and loved by all ages. It's quite normal for smart, suited businessmen to have a few favourite anime characters dangling from their phones!

You'll find cute characters and kawaii inspiration everywhere in Japan. Manga (comic books), anime (animated cartoons) and idols (singers and models) celebrate kawaii. Even serious institutions like the police and banks have kawaii mascots to help make everyday services feel more friendly!

ようこそ!

7

うれしいいいいいい

THE KAWAII ATTITUDE TO LIFE

Kawaii is about staying positive and adding some happiness to the world. Life seems a little easier when you're surrounded by happy faces or wearing bright colours and fun accessories.

Kawaii characters and manga/anime stories often focus on friendship, trying your best and the fact that life isn't always easy. Pusheen and Gudetama know that sometimes you just need to flop on the sofa with some snacks! Rilakkuma's thoughtful face looks sympathetic.

Kawaii fashion is about expressing your creativity and dressing in a way that makes you feel happy and confident, whatever anyone else thinks. Kawaii clothes and accessories make an outfit feel unique.

Your bedroom can become a cosy retreat with cute decorations and huggable plush where you can curl up with your favourite book or game. Even studying is much more fun with kawaii stationery, and mealtimes can be made sweeter with playful food, kawaii treats, bento-box lunches and animal-shaped utensils.

Once you start thinking kawaii, you'll find it will have a positive effect on just about everything!

世界中の友達を紹介しましょう！

MEET KAWAII'S INSPIRATIONAL ICONS!

Kawaii characters offer comfort, love and a happiness boost. They are loyal to their friends and family, and love adventures as much as being at home.

They often have baby-like features (both human and animal), such as large eyes and foreheads, round chubby bodies and small arms and legs. Their appearance might make them seem vulnerable but they are often brave and possess magic powers.

Even if you are new to kawaii, you have probably heard of the cute Pokémon, Pikachu. There are so many loveable mascots to discover. Turn the page to meet a few more from around the world and hear their stories…

DONUTELLA

The characters of the global lifestyle brand tokidoki were designed by Italian artist Simone Legno, and take inspiration from everything from Japanese culture to punk rock. Donutella whizzes around the galaxy in her donut UFO looking for sweet treats to fuel her friends. Everything tastes better with some sprinkles on top!

GUDETAMA

Japan-based Sanrio create their characters under the motto 'small gift, big smile'. Gudetama, the 'lazy egg', cannot help but bring a smile. Gudetama often lacks motivation and finds it hard to deal with life. If you can't get out bed in the morning, Gudetama totally understands.

HELLO KITTY

Hello Kitty was Sanrio's first creation. She is a true kawaii superstar. Never seen without her signature red bow, her motto for life is 'you can never have too many friends!' and she loves to play with other kawaii characters and brands. Make friends with her and she'll show you all the cutest new trends.

MIFFY THE RABBIT

A little white bunny in the garden inspired Dutch artist Dick Bruna to create Miffy for a series of picture books. Miffy enjoys every day adventures with her family and friends.

MOLANG

Molang was created by Hye-Ji Yoon, a Korean designer, for French studio Millimages. The animated series is an affectionate and humorous look at the relationship between an eccentric, joyful rabbit and a shy little chick. Despite their many differences, these two enjoy a unique friendship.

MOZZARELLA

Mozzarella is the head of tokidoki's Moofia family, who were assembled to extort milk from schoolyard bullies. Mozzarella is loving and kind to good kids, but feared by those who harass the innocent.

THE MOOMINS

The Moomins are some of the oldest kawaii characters, created by Finnish illustrator Tove Jansson in 1945. The adventurous family live in Moominvalley, where they explore and live in harmony with nature.

© MC™

THE OCTONAUTS

The Octonauts are a brave team (including Captain Barnacles, Peso, Dr Shellington, Professor Inkling, Kwazii, Dashi, Tweak and Tunip) that explore the undersea world. Created by Canadian design duo Meomi, this crew is always around to help out animals in need.

PUSHEEN

Pusheen is one of the world's most famous cats, gaining millions of fans since her origins in a web comic by American illustrator Claire Belton. As with most cats, she leads the ideal life: eating, sleeping, occasionally dressing up as a mermaid, unicorn and dinosaur, and spreading joy with her cheerful antics.

RICEMONSTERS

Take a trip to Ricetown, populated by British toy company Noodoll's cute plush monsters. Will you go shopping for happy fruit and veggies in the city with Riceananas, look after the farm or hang out in the jungle, desert or icy park? There is a Ricemonster for everyone.

RILAKKUMA

Rilakkuma, created by San X in Japan, translates as 'bear in relaxed mood'. Rilakkuma lives a totally stress-free life doing as little as possible – every day can be a lazy Sunday with Rilakkuma and friends, Korilakkuma (a white bear cub) and Kiiroitori (a yellow bird).

SMILING BEAR

Smiling Bear is Australia's cutest koala and thinks life is better when you smile more. Created by Guy Paterson, Smiling Bear hopes to raise global awareness and help protect real koalas while encouraging a positive outlook and a more relaxed life.

SUMIKKOGURASHI

Sumikkogurashi, from San-X, translates as 'things in the corner' and the shy misfit characters feel safe in the corner with others who understand what it's like to be the odd one out. The friends include Shirokuma, a shy bear who likes hot tea, Penguin?, a penguin with no self-confidence, and Tonkatsu, a fatty tonkatsu that no one wants to eat!

UNICORNO

Don't you wish you could visit the hidden kingdom of the Unicornos? The only way is through a magic waterfall that transformed these cute ponies into unicorns. The Unicornos, including Dolce, Pogo and Fumo, all live between the magical kingdom and our world.

KAWAII STYLE

KAWAII STYLE

Kawaii fashion is all about expressing your personality and making life fun. Wear whatever makes YOU happy and don't be afraid to experiment with different looks until you find your unique style.

Growing up doesn't mean you have to wear plain and boring clothes. Kawaii brands use bright colours, cute patterns, ruffles and bows that let you have fun at any age and show off your creativity and individuality.

Try layering colours and textures to build your outfit, whether it's pastels and lace frills for a sweet fairy style, denim and bold graphics for a colourful look, knits and velvet for cosy comfort or dark fabrics and glitter for some cosmic sparkle.

Accessories are the easiest way to cute up any outfit; draw attention with a big statement necklace or just add patterned tights or a fluffy hat. A fun bag will cheer you up every day; look for animal- and food-shaped designs or decorate a simple bag with your favourite pins, patches and hanging charms.

Take some inspiration from Harajuku street style and kawaii fashion icons and you'll soon be rocking your own cute looks.

WHAT'S YOUR KAWAII STYLE?

. . . .

Are you more Kurebayashi or Princess Peachie? Inspired more by Honey & Clover or Kyary Pamyu Pamyu? If you're not sure of your kawaii style yet, take this fun quiz to find out the perfect look and inspiration to suit your personality. Then turn to pages 122–23 to find out more about the brands to create each style.

Circle the answer that matches you best, then count them up to find your kawaii style. Try it on your friends too!

WHAT ARE YOUR FAVOURITE COLOURS?
1. Bright primary colours like red and yellow
2. Natural colours like green and turquoise
3. Pastel shades like pink and lavender
4. Bold colours like purple and silver

WHICH ANIMAL DO YOU MOST RESEMBLE?
1. A parrot – colourful and chatty
2. A rabbit – shy and fluffy
3. A unicorn – sparkly and magical
4. A black cat – playful and unconventional

WHAT'S YOUR FAVOURITE TIME OF YEAR?
1. Summer – sunshine, blue skies and holidays
2. Autumn – beautiful nature colours and cosy clothes
3. Spring – fresh flowers and Easter sweets
4. Halloween! You celebrate for the whole of October

WHAT ARE YOUR FAVOURITE SWEET TREATS?
1. Jelly beans
2. Fruit chews
3. Marshmallows
4. Gummy worms

WHAT WOULD BE YOUR DREAM HOLIDAY?
1. New York – lots of buzz and fun backgrounds for selfies
2. A cabin in the mountains where you can enjoy nature
3. Paris – romantic and dreamy with the prettiest sweet treats
4. A theme park so you can dress up and go on scary rides

ANSWERS

MOSTLY 1: COLOURFUL RAINBOW STYLE
If you love bright colours and find it hard to choose a favourite, Decora style is for you. With layers of colourful and patterned clothing, tons of cheap, fun accessories, and brightly coloured hair and make-up, you'll stand out in any crowd.

STYLE INSPIRATION:
Artist/model Kurebayashi and fashion label 6%DOKIDOKI.

MOSTLY 2: FOREST GIRL STYLE
If you're shy and love animals, you could be a Mori (Forest) Girl. Blend into nature with muted colours, oversized knits, fake fur, braids and animal-themed accessories.

STYLE INSPIRATION:
Honey & Clover anime and fashion label Franche Lippée.

MOSTLY 3: PASTEL FAIRY STYLE

If you dream of looking like a fairytale princess, try Fairy Kei or Sweet Lolita style. Start with the frilliest dress you can find and add ankle socks, mary-jane shoes, hair bows and sweets-themed jewellery.

STYLE INSPIRATION:
Artist/vlogger Princess Peachie and fashion label Baby, the Stars Shine Bright.

MOSTLY 4: CREEPY CUTE STYLE

If you wish it could be Halloween all year round, try the darker side of kawaii with Creepy Cute and Pastel Goth styles. Mix the frills, lace and pastels of lolita fashion with dark make-up, bat, bone or eyeball hair accessories, stripy tights and platform shoes.

STYLE INSPIRATION:
Singer/model Kyary Pamyu Pamyu and fashion label Listen Flavor.

NO CLEAR WINNER?

Try mixing and matching your favourite parts of each.

全部大好き!

Twinkie Chan

Jeanne

Julie

Kaila

女子のパワー

Amy

KAWAII
STREET STYLE!

You know your kawaii style, but how will you wear it?
Six kawaii girls share their favourite everyday looks,
brands and tips with us…

Lynsay

"Always look for bright colours, fun prints and little details like bows or ruffles. Even just a cute purse or hair clip can add a lot of personality to an outfit. Just have fun!"

Target for Boys

Lazy Oaf

Twinkie Chan

Target for Girls

Aggy Strap

NAME **Twinkie Chan**

OCCUPATION:
Crochet Designer & Social
Media Manager

LOCATION:
San Francisco, USA

INSTAGRAM:
@twinkiechan

URL:
www.twinkiechan.com

キラキラ光る
お空の星よ

HOW WOULD
YOU DESCRIBE
YOUR STYLE?

80s pastel cute
meets 90s grunge

WHAT ARE
YOUR FAVOURITE
KAWAII BRANDS?

Lazy Oaf, Fatally
Feminine

AMY'S STYLE IN FOCUS

Cakes with faces

Takeshita Street, Harajuku

Little Miss Delicious

ACDC Rag

Cutesy Kink

Cutesy Kink

Cutesy Kink

Converse

32

HOW WOULD YOU DESCRIBE YOUR STYLE?

Bright and colourful!

WHAT ARE YOUR FAVOURITE KAWAII BRANDS?

ACDC Rag, tokidoki

NAME **Amy**

OCCUPATION:
Designer & Vlogger

LOCATION:
Coventry, UK

INSTAGRAM:
@cakeswithfaces

URL:
www.cakeswithfaces.co.uk

"Wear what you love, and don't worry about what other people think!"

Japan Lover Me

Rainbowholic

Thrifted

NIKE

SUKAJAN
(SOUVENIR JACKET)

These embroidered satin jackets were originally commissioned by American soldiers in Japan at the end of the Second World War as a memory of their service. Vintage jackets are often unique but have inspired fashion brands to create their own more affordable designs.

NAME **Kaila**

OCCUPATION:
Blogger & Content Creator

LOCATION:
Saitama, Japan

INSTAGRAM:
@rainbowholic

URL:
www.rainbowholic.me

HOW WOULD
YOU DESCRIBE
YOUR STYLE?

Casual and comfy

WHAT ARE
YOUR FAVOURITE
KAWAII BRANDS?

Japan Lover Me,
ENJI

"Thrift stores are
the best places
to find unique
cute clothing!"

あの公園の
紅葉がきれい

35

JEANNE'S STYLE IN FOCUS

Forever 21!

Messy Pink

aimeekitty

Nile Perch x Sanrio

Storenvy

Angelic Pretty

36

Pastel, colourful,
frilly, fluffy...
everything cute!

WHAT ARE
YOUR FAVOURITE
KAWAII BRANDS?

Angelic Pretty,
Bonne Chance

NAME **Jeanne**

OCCUPATION:
Accessory Designer & Art
Curator

LOCATION:
Los Angeles, USA

INSTAGRAM:
@messypink

URL:
www.messypink.com

"Accessories, shirts, tights and
shoes can all be found for much
cheaper than the big lolita items
and you can find a lot of cute
pieces for cheap or on sale."

LoliMillie

Daiso

KOKOkim, Angelic Pretty, Barbie, Han Cholo, Miss Kika

No Bo

Angelic Pretty

Off-brand

tokidoki x London Sole

HOW WOULD
YOU DESCRIBE
YOUR STYLE?

Eclectic

WHAT ARE
YOUR FAVOURITE
KAWAII BRANDS?

Angelic Pretty,
Kreepsville 666

NAME **Julie**

OCCUPATION:
Artist

LOCATION:
Anaheim, USA

INSTAGRAM:
@aliendoll

"Frequent thrift stores,
yard sales and flea markets!
You never know what you're
going to find."

39

GAP

Ban.do

Not The Kind

Swoon Nails

Vintage

Vans

40

NAME **Lynsay**

OCCUPATION:
Life and Style Blogger

LOCATION:
Glasgow, UK

INSTAGRAM:
@lynsayloves

URL:
www.lynsayloves.com

"Mix together vintage, high street, designer and independent labels to concoct your own look."

HOW WOULD YOU DESCRIBE YOUR STYLE?

Colourful cartoon character meets retro glam

WHAT ARE YOUR FAVOURITE KAWAII BRANDS?

Tatty Devine, Isolated Heroes

MAKE KAWAII
WORK FOR YOU

. . . .

You might dream about going on a shopping spree in Harajuku, but if that's out of your budget there are plenty more affordable ways to find your perfect kawaii outfit.

HIGH STREET SHOPS

Kawaii style has started to filter down to the high street and you can find cute patterns and kawaii characters like Pusheen and Pikachu in stores like Primark and H&M. It's also worth checking the children's section in department stores and supermarkets – prices are cheaper than adult clothing and they get much cuter designs. T-shirts are often available in surprisingly large sizes and there's sure to be lots of colourful hair accessories and jewellery.

SECOND-HAND

If you can't afford the famous kawaii brands, keep an eye on auction sites like eBay and Buyee. You can find both used clothing and brand-new unwanted items at a fraction of the retail price. Just be careful to check the measurements and shipping costs and ask questions if you're not sure about something.

ETSY

Etsy is full of creative makers selling their own designs as clothing and accessories. You'll find a huge range of prices and styles and your money goes straight to the designer. Some will take custom or personalised orders too, so you can create something truly unique. Look out for indie designers at craft fairs and comic cons too.

SHOPPING FROM JAPAN

If you can't hop on a plane to Japan, this is the next best thing. While most Japanese online stores won't ship internationally, you can use a shopping service like Tenso as a go-between. You order as normal, giving the shipping service as your address, and they'll forward the order to you for an additional shipping cost.

MAKE IT YOURSELF!

If you enjoy crafts and can never find exactly what you want, try making your own clothes and accessories. Look out for beginner sewing classes at local craft shops and colleges or check out the millions of DIY videos on YouTube to learn how to make everything from resin jewellery to no-sew bags.

MAKE A FABRIC HAIR BOW

Georgie, founder of Beauxoxo, the UK-based hair accessories boutique, shows you how to make an easy, no-sew fabric bow. Turn it into a hair clip or headband, or attach to clothing.

- 20 x 30 cm (8 x 12 inches) fabric – thin cotton is ideal
- Glue gun or strong fabric glue
- Sewing thread or string
- Alligator clip or headband
- Small sharp scissors

TIP

No sewing skills are required, but you can replace the glue with stitching if you prefer

1

Mark a cross in the centre of the fabric.

2 Fold up one of the long sides to the centre cross and apply some hot glue along the whole length of fabric.

If you don't have a glue gun, you can use fabric glue, but allow extra time for the glue to dry.

3 Now fold over the other side of the fabric into the centre, overlapping it onto the glue line. Press together to secure.

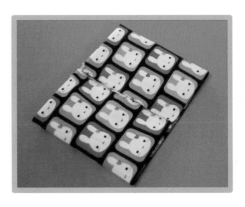

4

In a zig-zag motion, apply hot glue across the centre of the fabric piece. Fold the edges from each short side to meet in the centre and press together.

5

Gather down with the centre to create your bow shape and secure with some cotton or string.

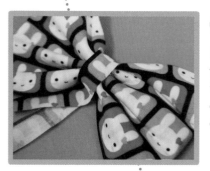

6

For the centre of the bow, cover with a smaller piece of the same fabric and glue in place. You could also use a matching or contrasting ribbon.

7

Attach an alligator clip to the back with the glue gun or another strip of fabric and it's ready to wear. You can also glue your bow onto a headband or sew onto clothing.

大きい毛の弓も好き

49

MAKE ANIMAL POM POM BAG CHARMS

Making these pom poms is easy and so addictive.
Here's how to make cute cat, bunny and fox pom poms
that you can hang from your bag or use as keyrings.

WHAT YOU'LL NEED

- Pom pom maker (see Tip below)
- Yarn
- Felt
- Long tapestry or sashiko needle
- Fabric glue or glue gun
- Small sharp scissors

TIP
You can use any
type of yarn – thin
yarn will take more time
but creates more detail,
while thick yarn is
faster and fluffier.

TIP
I find the wooden pom-
pom makers from Pom Maker
are easiest to use; Clover ones are
also the most widely available online
and in craft shops. If you don't want
to buy a pom pom maker, you can
simply cut out templates from card
(search "make pom poms with
cardboard" online for lots of
tutorials and templates).

1 Choose your favourite yarn colours and follow the instructions on your pom pom maker, wrapping the yarn on both sides, slotting the pieces together, cutting through the ends and tying tightly.

To make the animal designs, you can use one colour or add extra colours for fur markings. See the diagrams on page 57 for how much of each colour I used for a cat, bunny and fox. The fox can also double as a dog, so experiment with different colour combinations to match your own pet or favourite character.

2 Once removed from your pom pom maker, roll the pom pom in your hands to fluff it up into a ball. It will look really messy, but don't worry, it just needs a hair cut. Use your scissors to trim off small amounts of yarn all over your pom pom until it looks neat and round. It takes some time, and is very messy, but is definitely worth it for perfect pom poms.

3 As you trim, turn your pom pom around until you find the angle where the coloured markings create a face you like. Pay extra attention to those areas, trimming and pushing the strands to separate the colours. If the shapes aren't quite neat enough, you can pull out a few strands of yarn to tidy up the edges.

4 Thread your needle with a long piece of yarn or strong thread and push it through your pom pom from the top of the face to the bottom and then back to the top so that you have two ends of thread sticking out of the top. Remove the needle and tie the ends together in a knot twice, not too tightly. Leave the long ends un-cut for now.

Careful with the needle!

5. Draw face and ear shapes on coloured felt and cut them out. For layered pieces like ears, glue the pieces together with fabric glue, or pinch at the bottom and sew together for a 3D effect.

6. Try the felt pieces on your pom pom until you're happy with how it looks and then glue in place. For ears, push apart the pom pom strands to make a gap so you can place the ear far down and then squash the pom pom and ear together to fix in place.

7 Once dry, you can just use the loose ends to hang up your pom pom as a decoration, or else tie on a split ring, lobster clasp or elastic hairband for a more secure fastening for keys or bags.

よくできました!

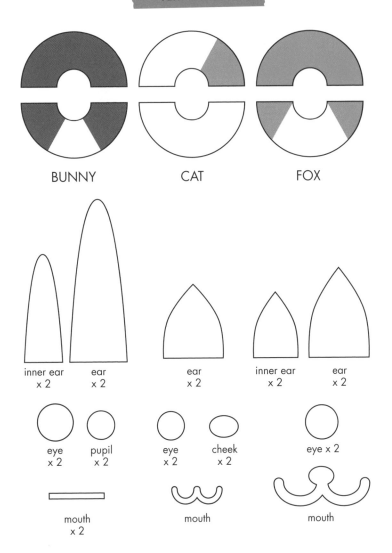

TEMPLATES

BUNNY   CAT   FOX

inner ear   ear   ear   inner ear   ear
x 2   x 2   x 2   x 2   x 2

eye   pupil   eye   cheek   eye x 2
x 2   x 2   x 2   x 2

mouth   mouth   mouth
x 2

57

nails

make-up

hair

Tokyo street style

パチッ

KAWAII
BEAUTY

If you can't commit to dyeing your hair, try wash-out hair chalk for that dreamy mermaid look. Add braids, bows or a cat ear headband for the best selfies.

Liquid eyeliner, an eyelash curler and lots of mascara will help get you those big dolly eyes. Match them with pastel shades and a bit of glitter for a super sweet look. Don't forget your nails – try alternating different colours of polish and add some fun nail stickers for the perfect finishing touch.

RAINBOW HAIR

· ·

If you're not allowed to dye your hair bright colours, or just can't decide on one, there are some great temporary options to play with at the weekend and wash out by Monday morning.

HAIR CHALKS & SPRAYS

Hair chalks and coloured hairsprays are widely available, easy to apply and wash out quickly. They work on all hair colours so you can use pastels for a dreamy mermaid feel, bright colours for rainbow hair or get the ombre style by just adding colour to the ends.

SEMI-PERMANENT DYE

If you're thinking about dyeing your hair, or want a change on holiday, semi-permanent dyes are perfect. There's a huge range of colours available on the high street and they only last for 4–12 washes, so you can see if you like it before making a final decision.

どう？似合う？

WIGS

If you wish you had completely different hair, wigs are the easy way to do it. Whether you go for something low key or OTT, you can have long hair, curls or a rainbow of colours. Wigs are available online and from specialist shops in a variety of styles and colours. Kanekalon and toyokalon wigs are fine for cosplay and selfies, but if you want to wear your wig regularly, look for more realistic monofilament wigs.

HAIR FASHION IN HARAJUKU

MAKE-UP INSPIRATION

· ·

Make-up is fun to experiment with and can bring
your whole look together.

EVERYDAY MAKE-UP
For everyday, keep things soft and fresh. Use pastel shades
on eyes, lips and cheeks and eyelash curlers to open up your
eyes. A little bit of shimmer can add some fun too. If you're
out in the sun, don't forget to protect your skin with a high SPF.

PARTY TIME
For a special event or party, you can really go wild. Use
bolder and brighter colours and try glitter eyeshadow, metallic
lipstick, fake eyelashes or coloured mascara to stand out from
the crowd. For a super colourful look, follow the Decora style
and add stickers and transfers below your eyes.

COSPLAY
For cosplay, try contact lenses with different colours and
patterns, available online. They enlarge your pupils to make
you look like an anime character! If you're wearing a wig
or have coloured your hair, match your eyebrows with
eyeshadow and mascara.

KAWAII BRANDS

You can use any brands that work for you, but for extra special colours head online. Indie brands like Sugarpill and Limecrime create the coolest colours that are animal-friendly too. Korea leads the world in cute make-up and skincare with packaging that is so kawaii you'll want it all. Search out Tony Moly and Etude House for products that look like animals, sweets and ice cream.

Remember that kawaii style is whatever makes you happy, so have fun, experiment and don't worry about what other people think. If you decide make-up isn't something you enjoy, you can still be kawaii without it.

SUPER CUTE NAILS

· ·

Decorating your nails is an easy and fun way to add
an extra touch of cute to your outfit.

NAIL POLISH
You don't need to spend a lot of money to get cute nails. Try
painting each nail a different colour for a quirky look or use
two colours on the same nail in stripes or shapes.

There are also lots of fun nail polishes available on the high
street that are mixed with swirls of colour, glitter pieces and
even unicorn shapes. Layer over dark colours for galaxy style
or over pastels for sweet sparkles.

*Use washi tape to help you paint
shapes and straight lines –
it peels off easily after.*

NAIL TRANSFERS

Transfers (also called decals) are a quick way to add something different to your nails. Search on Etsy for kawaii designs featuring everything from animals to food. You just paint on a base colour, cut out a transfer and use a damp sponge to apply it to your nail.

Nail transfers by Pearl Planet

A clear top coat will protect the design and keep it looking cute for longer.

NAIL WRAPS

Nail wraps are thin vinyl sheets that are heat-sensitive, so you only need a hairdryer for long-lasting nails. There's a wide range of patterns available online and in shops that fit all nail sizes and lengths.

CUSTOM NAIL ART

For a special occasion, you need a professional, and nail salons will usually be happy to work with you on a custom design. Bring along one of my ideas, your favourite character or your own design for unique nails that will get a lot of attention.

Burger
choose your own toppings and
don't forget the sesame seeds

Rainbow
stripe your favourite colours or
use the whole rainbow set

Clouds
the fluffier the better, so don't
worry about getting them perfect

Bow
try red on gold glitter for a
Christmas party

Ghost
a spooky cute look that's perfect for Halloween

Watermelon
make your nails look fresh for summer beach trips

Sprinkles
make it look like you've dipped your fingers in cupcake frosting

Panda
change the colours and eyes for a teddy bear or polar bear

KAWAII, TOKYO-STYLE

Welcome to the kawaii capital of the world! Tokyo is a huge city with so many kawaii shops and sights that it's impossible to see it all in one trip. Luckily, there's an area dedicated to kawaii where you can visit lots of the cutest brands, shops and cafés in one day:

HARAJUKU

So let's take a shopping tour together around the magical district of Harajuku. Many international fashion trends start here as fashion students, designers and teenagers show off their outfits for the roaming street style photographers of FRUiTS and TokyoFashion.com.

KAWAII STREET STYLE IN HARAJUKU

一緒に原宿へ行こう!

TAKESHITA STREET ENTRANCE

Start on TAKESHITA STREET – Harajuku's kawaii fashion shopping street and easy to find opposite JR Harajuku station. New stores pop up all the time to show off the latest trends and crazes, so keep your eyes open. For fashion, look out for ACDC RAG, SPINNS, LIZ LISA, WEGO and the ALTA mini mall plus second-hand brands at CLOSET CHILD. ETUDE HOUSE sells the cutest Korean beauty products or visit DAISO for beauty bargains.

DAISO IN HARAJUKU

MARION CREPES

Refuel at MARION CREPES (a Harajuku staple) and don't forget to document your outfit with PURIKURA – photo booths with Snapchat-style filters.

プリクラ

マリオンクレープ

PURIKURA FUN WITH FRIENDS

Next stop: LAFORET. This department store is dedicated to Harajuku fashion, with six floors of big-name designers, independent brands and pop-up shops. You can even book a photo session at MAISON DE JULIETTA to dress up in full Sweet Lolita style.

LAFORET

You can't miss the bright-pink boutique 6%DOKIDOKI, showcasing kawaii designer Sebastian Masuda's clothing, while BABY, THE STARS SHINE BRIGHT offers beautifully detailed Lolita dresses, accessories and stationery.

CATWALK AT BABY, THE STARS SHINE BRIGHT

原宿

6%DOKIDOKI

皆田セバスチャーリ

SEBASTIAN MASUDA

Sebastian Masuda is one of the biggest names in Harajuku kawaii culture. Creating art from layers of toys, plastic and candy in eye-popping colours, his designs can be seen all around Harajuku. Look out for fashion boutique 6%DOKIDOKI, the Kawaii Monster Café and the Moshi Moshi Box kawaii tourist information centre.

For a super kawaii meal, head to the KAWAII MONSTER CAFÉ for rainbow pasta, "poisonous" parfaits and colourful mocktails. Created by artist and fashion designer Sebastian Masuda, it's like stepping into one of his Kyary Pamyu Pamyu music videos.

Or, for something sweeter, the POMPOMPURIN CAFÉ is themed around Sanrio's pudding dog character with adorable decor and a full menu of main meals, desserts, snacks and drinks, all shaped and decorated to look like the character.

Once you're recharged, head to KIDDYLAND, possibly the greatest kawaii store in the world. Imagine a shop dedicated to all your favourite kawaii characters with six floors of cute plush, stationery, accessories, kitchenware and much more.

CURRY AT POMPOMPURIN CAFÉ

GUDETAMA KEYRINGS
IN KIDDYLAND

PLUSH TOYS IN KIDDYLAND

On your way back to the station, stop and visit the cats at MOCHA CAT CAFÉ. Most Japanese homes are too small for pets, so cat cafés let you spend some time playing and relaxing with the café cats. MoCHA has especially stylish decor for the cutest photos and includes unlimited drinks and cat-shaped snacks.

OUTSIDE OF HARAJUKU

While Harajuku is home to most of the kawaii hotspots, there are a few other areas that are well worth exploring.

CHARACTER STREET

Character Street is handily situated in the basement of Tokyo Station. You'll find shops dedicated to Hello Kitty, Rilakkuma, Studio Ghibli, Miffy, Pokémon, Sumikko Gurashi and more, with exclusive products and special souvenirs. Just around the corner is the KITKAT CHOCOLATORY and OKASHI LAND, where you can stock up on Japanese treats including limited-edition seasonal flavours of Pocky and KitKats.

POKEMON CENTER

キャラクターストリート

KITKAT CHOCOLATORY

Shibuya is just one station along from Harajuku and great for kawaii shopping. LOFT is stationery heaven and also sells cute homeware and character goods. TOKYU HANDS has supplies for all kinds of craft projects plus some weird and wonderful souvenirs. Stop at ITS 'DEMO to see their latest kawaii character collaboration on beauty and fashion goods. SWEETS PARADISE is a dessert café where you have an hour to try as many of the pretty cakes and puddings as you can manage!

CUTE STATIONERY AT LOFT

渋谷

WEIRD SOUVENIR
AT TOKYU HANDS

AKIHABARA BY NIGHT

秋葉原

UFO CATCHER

SUPER POTATO

If you love anime or video games, you can't miss out on **Akihabara**. This area is famous for otaku (geek) culture and is a collector's dream. Pick up anime figures at ASO BIT CITY, browse the retro Nintendo games at SUPER POTATO or try your luck with the UFO CATCHERS at the arcades for rare plush and merchandise. You can even eat like your favourite anime character at ANIMATE CAFÉ or visit one of the animal cafés to hang out with cats, rabbits or owls!

CUTE,
COSY
LIVING

つがいが大切です

CUTE, COSY LIVING

Whether you have a huge bedroom to yourself, or just a small space of your own, it's easy to turn it into a happy place for you to relax.

Bright colours like yellow and orange can boost your mood. Natural colours like green and lavender are calming. White backgrounds make colourful decorations pop, while darker colours like purple are cosy and luxurious. For a really fun look, try painting rainbow stripes on one wall!

If you collect cute things, get them out on display so you can enjoy them all the time. Plush or figures can be arranged on shelves and a display shelf with compartments is perfect for small toys and miniatures. Favourite jewellery and pins can be displayed on a corkboard or fabric banner.

Even studying can be more fun when you have pretty stationery and a personalised planner to keep you on track. If you find it hard to keep things tidy, plain boxes, jars and pots can be decorated with patterned paper, paint and stickers.

Add some cosy bedding and cushions and you'll never want to leave!

MAKE
A KAWAII HAVEN

• •

Posters, garlands and framed art will add some interest to your walls, and you could even add a few hooks to show off favourite dresses and bags. For an easy feature wall, hang a large piece of patterned fabric above your bed or desk.

Bedding can make a big difference to your room and there are lots of cute patterns and character sets available online and on the high street. Look out for reversible designs to give you extra options or mix and match the pillowcases from different sets.

A cosy blanket and a pile of colourful cushions will make your bed a comfy retreat where you can curl up with a book or TV show. Fluffy rugs also keep things cosy and add some fun texture.

Overhead lighting can be harsh, so choose a few different lighting sources that you can use depending on your mood. An angled desk light is great for studying and crafting, while fairy lights and colour-changing lamps will help you relax at night.

Plants like succulents and cacti are easy to care for and will look cute in pots decorated with stickers or paint.

For a final touch, add a scented candle with a sweet fragrance. Fruity and floral scents are widely available or search on Etsy for fun scents like jelly beans and candy floss!

START A
KAWAII JOURNAL

Journals are a fun, creative hobby that can also help you
to stay organised and store your dreams and memories.

BULLET JOURNAL

A bullet journal is a mix of diary, to-do list and goal tracking with pages you customise to suit your life. A dotted or squared notebook makes it easy to draw your own layouts and calendars but any notebook will do with the help of stencils or squares of paper. Use coloured pens and symbols to mark regular tasks, activities or chores on a weekly or monthly calendar to keep on track. Add separate areas for a to-do list and tick off daily goals.

Decorate with cute washi tape and stickers to inspire you.

DAILY JOURNAL

If you prefer something less structured, journalling is a relaxing hobby that results in a creative memory book of your life. Use a page-a-day diary or blank notebook and let your creativity run wild. Write down the day's main events, create a collage that fits your mood, or draw your outfit or meals. Think how much fun it will be to have a record of your year.

TRAVEL JOURNAL

If you have a big trip planned, a travel journal will give you something to look back on to remember all the fun you had. Use it before the trip to plan everything from your top places to visit to your packing list, then bring it with you to jot down the day's events. When you get home, you can stick in reminders of your trip like entry tickets, postcards and photographs and write about or draw your favourite sights, meals and adventures.

KAILA FILLS HER JOURNAL WITH HAPPY MEMORIES

CHICHI KEEPS A DAILY ILLUSTRATED JOURNAL OF HER LIFE

88

DONUT GARLAND

These yummy treats will look super cute hanging above a desk or bed.

- Coloured card
- Pair of compasses
- Scissors
- Glue
- String or ribbon
- Tape or small pegs
- Pens and decorations

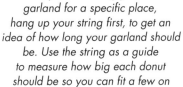

TIP
If you're making your garland for a specific place, hang up your string first, to get an idea of how long your garland should be. Use the string as a guide to measure how big each donut should be so you can fit a few on the garland. Otherwise, just draw them any size you like.

 1

Draw donut shapes on coloured
card with a pair of compasses.
Draw one large circle and then
a smaller circle from the same
point. Cut them out.

2 For icing, draw the same donut shape but then draw
a wavy line inside the outer circle before cutting out.

 3

Decorate your donuts with
confetti, mini pom poms,
glitter glue or coloured pens.

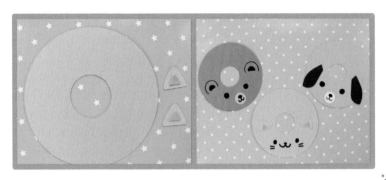

4 For animal donuts, you can either draw on the features or cut them from card for a 3D effect.

5

When your donuts are dry, attach them to the string with small pegs or washi tape. You could even clip them to LED string lights for extra fun.

You can also make individual donuts to stick on cards or use as place settings for a party.

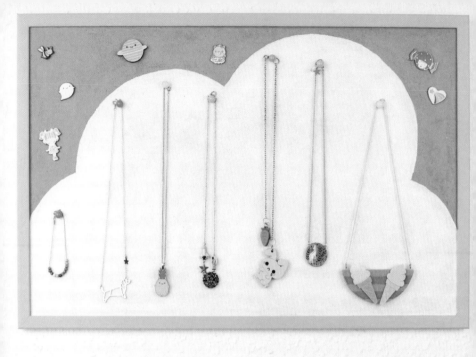

JEWELLERY DISPLAY BOARD

If your necklaces are getting tangled up or forgotten in a drawer, put them on display so you can enjoy them every day.

- A cork board, as big as your longest necklace chain
- Acrylic paint
- Paintbrush
- Pencil
- Pins (fun colours and animal designs)
- Hanging kit (included with most cork boards) or Command strips

TIP
Stationery stores have so many cute pin styles including animals, food and a rainbow of colours.

TIP
Corkboards are widely available online, or try office supply stores and IKEA.

Draw guidelines for your design onto the cork board with a pencil. A cloud is easy – just draw circles using a small plate – but you could do rainbow stripes or a cat face or anything else you like.

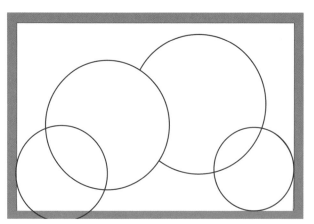

You can use the above as a guide to how to draw a cloud shape with plates!

2 Place the cork board on top of a box or two piles of books to lift it up and then paint the frame. Doing this first means it doesn't matter if you get some paint on the cork. Paint around the sides too for a professional look. You may need a second coat.

3 Now move on to your design. Use a small, flat brush to get paint under the edge of the frame and work from dark colours to light. You'll probably need two or three coats of paint to cover the cork completely.

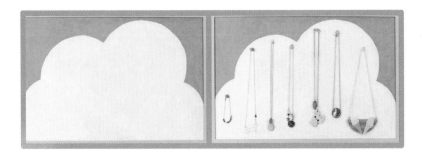

4 Once the paint is dry, lay out your necklaces and bracelets on the board until you have a nice display, then mark lightly where the pins should go. Remove all the jewellery before hanging up your display board – take a photo for reference if you might forget what goes where.

5 Either follow the instructions included with the board for hanging with nails or use removable Command strips. Once it's securely on the wall, you can add the pins and hang your jewellery up. Place brooches and enamel pins in the spaces by pinning them straight into the cork.

To make sure your board is straight, ask a friend or family member to help or use a spirit level.

JEWELLERY FROM HZ.CO.UK

ステキー

HAPPY FOOD!

HAPPY FOOD!

One of my favourite things about visiting Japan is how cute all the food is! From animal-shaped donuts to perfectly decorated cakes, everything makes you reach for your camera.

Many kawaii food ideas originated with Japanese bento boxes. Parents often add cute touches to their children's lunch boxes with hot dogs cut into octopus shapes, or rice moulded to look like a favourite character with faces cut from nori seaweed or cheese.

Bento supplies are available online from sites like Bento&co and BentoUSA and can help make everyday meals more kawaii. Rice moulds are great for onigiri rice balls and curry, and vegetable cutters can even make salad more appealing.

Character cafés are one of the cutest food trends in Japan just now and have started to spread worldwide too. Themed around a kawaii character, game or anime, they have a full menu of meals, snacks and drinks that look like the characters, plus cute decor. If you can't visit one in person, use them as inspiration to make a party extra special.

Whatever you try, mealtimes are sure to get a little cuter!

KAWAII TREATS TO TRY

• •

Japan has created some of the cutest snacks around, with fun
flavours and kawaii packaging. Here are a few famous brands to
look out for. They're widely available online from shops like Tofu
Cute and in Asian supermarkets.

POCKY

Pocky are biscuit sticks covered
in chocolate and come in lots of
flavours, from strawberry and
banana to pumpkin and tiramisu.
There are special editions too,
including heart-shaped Pocky
sticks for Valentine's Day and
giant Pocky sticks 8 inches long!

KITKATS

KitKats are popular in Japan as good-
luck gifts as the name is similar to
"Kitto Katsu" ("You will surely win" in
Japanese). There have been over 300
flavours so far, from apple to sweet
potato, plus bakeable KitKats that you
grill in the oven.

MILKY

Milky is a classic Japanese brand that has been around since 1951. The caramel candy is made with famously creamy Hokkaido milk and the packaging features their cute mascot, Peko-chan.

POPIN' COOKIN'

These DIY candy kits are filled with powders, moulds and tools to help you make tiny edible treats. The details are incredible and you can make everything from pizza and burgers to donuts and ice cream.

KOALA'S MARCH

These biscuits don't just have kawaii packaging – each biscuit is in the shape of a koala with a cute design stamped on top. Inside is a fondant filling with flavours including chocolate, strawberry and matcha green tea.

UNICORN TOAST

Make breakfast time more magical with this sparkly pastel treat.

WHAT YOU'LL NEED

- Slice of bread
- Light cream cheese
- Food colouring
- Unicorn sprinkles (available online and in supermarkets)

TIP
You can make your own unicorn sprinkles by mixing together different colours and sizes of sprinkles and candy.

Add a teaspoon of cream cheese into two (or more!) small bowls and add food colouring. Start with just a drop at a time and mix thoroughly to create your favourite pastel shades.

Toast your bread on both sides and place on a cute plate.

For a healthier version, use yogurt mixed with a little honey and natural food colourings like matcha tea, turmeric and beetroot.

Use a flat knife to spread your coloured cream cheese onto the toast. You can do half and half, stripes, or swirl the colours together.

4 Decorate with sprinkles! Start with a layer of the smallest sprinkles then add larger pieces individually.
Take a photo and enjoy!

APPLE BUNNIES

These cute bunnies make for a healthy snack and will add some kawaii to your five a day. All you need is an apple and a sharp knife.

- 1 apple
- Edible sprinkles
- A little milk or white chocolate or icing sugar

TIP

Dip your bunnies into water with a little lemon juice or salt added to keep them from turning brown.

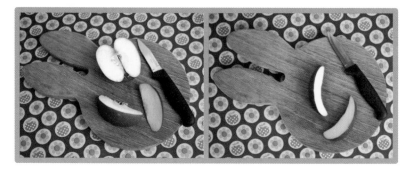

1. Cut your apple in half from top to bottom, then cut in half twice more until you have eight slices. Remove the core.

2

Take each slice and cut a V shape into the skin, as shown. Don't cut too deeply into the apple.

Peel away the skin by cutting just underneath with your knife from the back of the apple to the point where your ears join, as shown. The skin should peel away easily – if not, cut your ear shapes a little deeper.

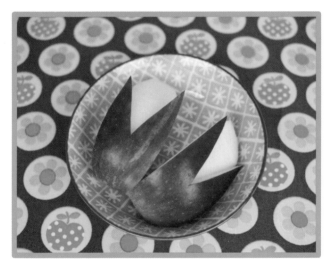

You can also add small sprinkles for eyes – just use a little melted chocolate or icing sugar mixed with water to attach them.

111

RAINBOW CUPCAKES

These colourful cupcakes will wow your friends
and are surprisingly easy to make.

- Box of light-coloured cake mix
- Food colouring
- Silicone cupcake pan (or metal tin with paper cases)
- 140g/5oz butter, softened*
- 280g/10oz icing sugar*
- 2 tbsp milk*
(*or premade frosting)
- Piping bag or plastic food bag
- Sprinkles

TIP
*If you buy red, blue
and yellow colouring,
you can mix them
together to create
more colours.*

Preheat oven to 180°C/350°F/ Gas Mark 4.
Make the cake mix according to the instructions and divide equally into small bowls – one for each colour.
Add food colouring to each bowl to create a rainbow of colours. Start with just a drop at a time and mix thoroughly until you get the shades you want. Use small amounts for pastel colours and more for bright colours.

Add a teaspoon from each colour of batter to your cupcake tin. You can dollop in the colours randomly, spread into layers or hide a colour in the middle.

To check the cakes are cooked, insert a knife or toothpick and it should come out cleanly with no wet batter.

3 Place on a low shelf in the oven to prevent browning and bake for 15–25 minutes until the tops are rounded.

4

Remove the cupcakes from the tin and leave to cool completely.

5. Add the butter to a large bowl and beat until soft. Add half of the icing sugar and continue beating until smooth, then add the rest of the icing sugar and repeat. If the icing is too stiff to pipe, add a little milk to loosen it. Spoon into a piping bag or use a small plastic food bag and cut off the corner. Ice your cupcakes in any pattern you like, then decorate with sprinkles.

There are so many fun sprinkles available online and at supermarkets. Look out for glitter, rainbow, metallic or star-shaped sprinkles, or mix them all together.

いただきます！

117

DISCOVER MORE KAWAII!

• •

Don't let your kawaii adventure end here – there is a world of cuteness waiting to be explored, from fun shopping to brilliant games…

SHOPPING

While the internet has made it easy to shop for kawaii anywhere in the world, it's really nice to shop in person. These are the ten best shops to visit around the world…

Kiddyland (Tokyo, Japan)

The most kawaii shop in the world, full of cute characters (see page 73).

ARTBOX (London, UK)

Tucked away in London's Covent Garden area, this tiny shop can be spotted from quite a distance due to the cute window displays! Inside you'll find character goods from all your favourite Japanese brands, along with mini concessions from sister shops Tofu Cute (candy and plush) and Dreamy Bows (Japanese fashion).

JapanLA (Los Angeles, USA)

JapanLA would be worth visiting just for their huge range of character goods, but they also collaborate with kawaii brands for their own super cute products and clothing. Look out for exclusive items featuring Rilakkuma, Pokémon, Totoro and more.

Tofu Cute (Portsmouth, UK)

You might not think of Portsmouth as a top destination for kawaii, but it's home to one of the cutest shops in the world. Tofu Cute's adorable pink shop is crammed full of Japanese candy, Amuse plush and all those cute little bits and pieces that are impossible to resist.

Loft (Tokyo, Japan)
This is stationery heaven (see page 76)!

Queenie's Cards (Toronto, Canada)
Canadians can get their kawaii fix at this new store run by kawaii illustrator Queenie. You'll find her original characters and designs alongside popular characters like Pusheen, tokidoki and Gudetama.

A Little Lovely Company (Netherlands)
You might not recognise any of the characters in this Dutch chain but you'll soon fall in love with their original designs. Your room will be much cuter with a happy cloud lamp, popsicle string lights or rainbow shelf.

Daiso (Japan, USA & Asia)
If you were shopping for kawaii, you probably wouldn't head to the nearest pound shop, but it's quite a different matter in Japan. Daiso sells a wide range of products, from stationery and craft supplies to beauty products and candy, all priced under ¥300. They're also expanding worldwide, so look out for branches across the USA and Asia.

Sanrio Stores (Worldwide)
You can find Sanrio stores all around the world selling cute character goods featuring Hello Kitty and friends. Serious fans will dream of visiting the flagship store in Tokyo's Ginza district, which promises the world's largest array of Sanrio products, with limited-edition collaborations and exclusive regional items.

Character Street (Tokyo, Japan)
If time is tight in Japan, this street of shops is the best pitstop to make to top up on your favourite kawaii brands (see page 75).

And for those times you can't get to a store, you have all of these shops online to explore...

KEY

🐱 character

╲ stationery

★ fashion

🎀 beauty

🍙 food

⛰ home

TIP
Stores will ship internationally but choose one near you to save on shipping and import fees.

AmiAmi (Japan)
www.amiami.com 🐱 ╲ ⛰

Beauty Bay (UK)
www.beautybay.com 🎀

BeautyNetKorea (Korea)
www.beautynetkorea.com 🎀

Beauxoxo (UK)
www.beauxoxo.com ★

Bento&co (Japan)
en.bentoandco.com 🍙 ⛰

Bento USA (USA)
www.bentousa.com 🍙 ⛰

Cakes With Faces (UK)
www.cakeswithfaces.co.uk ★

Cutesy Kink (UK)
www.cutesykink.co.uk 🐱 ★

Dolls Kill (USA)
www.dollskill.com ★

Dreamy Bows (UK)
www.dreamybows.com ★ ⋈

Etsy (Worldwide)
www.etsy.com 🐱 \ ★ ⋈ 🏔

Hannah Zakari (UK)
www.hannahzakari.co.uk \ ★ 🏔

Hot Topic (USA)
www.hottopic.com 🐱 ★

IT'SUGAR (USA)
www.itsugar.com 🐱 🍙

J-List (Japan)
www.jlist.com 🐱 🍙 🏔

Japan Centre (UK)
www.japancentre.com 🍙 🏔

JetPens (USA)
www.jetpens.com \

Kawaii Panda (Portugal)
kawaii-panda.com 🐱 \ ⋈ 🍙

Lush (Worldwide)
www.lush.com ⋈

Modes4U (Hong Kong)
www.modes4u.com 🐱 \ 🏔

Paperchase (UK)
www.paperchase.co.uk 🐱 \ ⋈ 🏔

Pusheen Shop (USA)
www.pusheen.com 🐱 ★

Rainbowholic Shop (Japan)
www.rainbowholic-shop.com \

Smoko (USA)
www.smokonow.com 🏔

Sock It To Me (USA)
www.sockittome.com ★

Sugarpill (USA)
www.sugarpill.com ⋈

Tasty Peach Studios (USA)
www.tastypeachstudios.com 🐱 ★

Tokyo Otaku Mode (Japan)
www.otakumode.com 🐱 ★ 🏔

Tony Moly (USA)
www.tonymoly.us ⋈

YesStyle (Hong Kong) ★ ⋈
www.yesstyle.com

For more shops, check out Super Cute Kawaii's Shopping Guide
http://www.supercutekawaii.com/super-cute-shopping-guide/

Here is a list of my favourite kawaii brands to look out for too...

6%DOKIDOKI
The original Harajuku kawaii brand is an explosion of colour. Their clothing and accessories feature detailed collages by founder and artist Sebastian Masuda, who also designs singer Kyary Pamyu Pamyu's stage sets.

ACDC Rag
Combining all the many styles of Harajuku fashion, this pop punk brand stands out with bright colours and bold graphics.

Angelic Pretty
The oldest Lolita fashion brand was founded in 1979 and is still creating clothing fit for a princess, with layers of ruffles, lace and ribbons.

Baby, The Stars Shine Bright
One of the biggest names in Lolita fashion that was featured in the film *Kamikaze Girls*. Their dresses are intricately detailed with a fairytale theme.

Chocomint
The cutest hair accessories and jewellery for Sweet Lolita and Fairy Kei outfits, with everything from fluffy sweets to sparkly tulle bows.

Galaxxxy
This colourful brand has a cool retro style with bright colours and cartoon graphics and has collaborated with everyone from model Rin Rin Doll to Adventure Time.

Listen Flavor
Their casual fashions look cute and sweet on the surface but also have a dark edge, making them perfect for Pastel Goth, Decora and Pop Punk outfits.

Liz Lisa
A sweet girly brand with floral and candy designs and lots of lace, ribbons and fake fur. They regularly partner with Sanrio's My Melody for adorable clothing collaborations.

Q-pot
Realistic and detailed sweets jewellery that looks good enough to eat. Their flagship store in Harajuku even has a café serving edible versions.

Tokyo Bopper
Proudly made in Japan, their signature thick-soled high platform shoes will make you stand out in any crowd with styles that suit all looks.

SUBSCRIPTION BOXES
If you love getting surprises in the mail, these regular mystery boxes are packed full of cuteness.

Sanrio Small Gift Crate
A quarterly box full of all-exclusive items featuring Hello Kitty and friends. Previous boxes have been themed around food, beach holidays and friendship. lootcrate.com/crates/sanrio

YumeTwins
The YumeTwins Team are always looking for the cutest trends around Harajuku to fill their monthly boxes. Expect a mix of plush, stationery, accessories and homeware featuring top kawaii characters. yumetwins.com

Japan Crate
If you like to try new flavours, these monthly boxes are filled with weird and wonderful Japanese candy, snacks, drinks and DIY kits that are fun to share with friends. japancrate.com

nomakenolife
If you sometimes feel you couldn't live without make-up, this is the box for you! Each monthly box includes a selection of Japanese beauty products and accessories to add to your routine. nomakenolife.com

Pipsticks
You can never have enough stickers, and Pipsticks will keep your collection growing. Each monthly package contains 15 sheets plus printables and extras. pipsticks.com

TOP KAWAII EVENTS

Kawaii events and conventions are great places to meet up with fellow kawaii fans and anime geeks while wearing your cutest outfit or cosplay. There are events worldwide but these are some of the biggest.

Hyper Japan

The cutest event in the UK is held in London twice a year and there's so much to do! Enjoy performances by Japanese pop groups and Japanese films or get involved in the fashion shows and craft classes. There's plenty of shopping opportunities from UK kawaii shops and designers of all sizes plus the chance to try some Japanese snacks.
hyperjapan.co.uk

CatCon

If you love cats, imagine a whole event dedicated to cats! At CatCon, held in Pasadena, USA, you can meet celebrity cats, check out panel discussions, shop for cute products for you and your cat and even adopt a real cat to take home.
catconworldwide.com

San Diego Comic Con

There are hundreds of Comic Con events worldwide but San Diego is the biggest of the lot and an experience you'll never forget. So big that it's impossible to see everything, there will be something amazing around every corner, with exclusive merchandise, incredible costumes, and actors and artists from your favourite comic books and movies.
comic-con.org

Design Festa

Anyone can apply for this twice-yearly art and design event, held in Tokyo, so it's a real mix of stalls and styles that will fill you with inspiration. With areas dedicated to art, design and fashion, you can browse handmade toys, illustrated zines, unique outfits and futuristic prototypes.
designfesta.com/en

YOUTUBE CHANNELS

Pick up a new hobby or get a peek into the kawaii lifestyle with these cute vloggers.

Bunny+Me Show

Learn to draw in the kawaii style with this cute bunny.
www.youtube.com/user/bunnyandmeshow

Cakes With Faces

Join Amy as she travels around Japan's coolest sights.
www.youtube.com/user/cakeswithfaces

Flying Mio

Cute DIY crafts of every kind from crochet to clay.
www.youtube.com/user/flyingmiomio

Kawaii Sweet World

The cutest recipes for edible sweet treats plus foodie crafts.
www.youtube.com/user/kawaiisweetworld

Maqaroon

The latest kawaii crazes with easy crafts, slime and recipes.
www.youtube.com/user/maqaroon

Paper Kawaii

Learn to make just about anything out of paper with these origami tutorials.
www.youtube.com/user/paperkawaii/

Princess Peachie

Kawaii lifestyle and fashion with Sweet Lolita icon Peachie.
www.youtube.com/user/PeachieAngelPrincess

Rainbowholic TV

Kaila's daily journalling inspiration and kawaii life in Japan.
www.youtube.com/user/rainbowholicTV

TheHollycopter

Kawaii unboxings, reviews and tutorials.
www.youtube.com/user/TheHollycopter

Tokyo Fashion

The latest street fashion and beauty straight from Harajuku.
www.youtube.com/user/TokyoFashionNews

MOBILE GAMES

These cute free games will keep you entertained on the go, whether you're on iPhone or Android.

Animal Crossing: Pocket Camp

Start a new life in a camper van and build your own cute campsite while making friends with a cast of loveable animal characters.

Dr Moku

If learning Japanese is one of your ambitions, these fun apps will help you quickly learn the alphabets with cartoon memory tricks that really work.

Neko Atsume

Collect all the cats! Leave out toys and food in your virtual garden and soon lots of cute cats will start to visit and leave you gifts. Look out for extra special rare cats too.

Pokémon GO

Get outside and search for Pikachu and friends in the real world. This game makes your hometown seem much more exciting, with new Pokémon appearing all the time.

SUMI SUMI

An extra cute puzzle game that features San-X characters, including Rilakkuma and Sumikkogurashi.

For more cute shops, characters, DIYS, reviews and giveaways, visit us at Super Cute Kawaii!
www.supercutekawaii.com | @sckawaii

Thank you to the following for use of photos and additional help:
Amy Crabtree, Andrea Mahovetz, Billy Smith, Chichi Romero, Claire Brown, Fiona Dulieu, Georgie Foster, Guy Paterson, Jan Brown, Jeanne Trejo, Julie Doll, Kaila Ocampo, Kendy Paxia, Lynsay Neil, Meomi Design, Mercis BV, Millimage, Moomin Characters, Natasja Capelle, Nicolette Smith, Noodoll Ltd, Paulina Honig, Pusheen, Rachael Griffiths, Sanrio, San-X, TofuCute.com, Tokidoki and Twinkie Chan.

10 9 8 7 6 5 4 3 2 1

Published in 2019 by Pop Press an imprint of Ebury Publishing,
20 Vauxhall Bridge Road, London SW1V 2SA

Pop Press is part of the Penguin Random House group of companies
whose addresses can be found at global.penguinrandomhouse.com

Penguin
Random House
UK

Always follow your heart

楽しかったね！
またねー